MW01633893

# I Believe

## The Apostles' Creed in Sacred Art for Young Children

BY KERRI DAVISON

HOLY HEROES BOOKS

HolyHeroes.com

Dedicated with gratitude
to parents and grandparents
who pass on the deep wisdom of the Faith
by reading to little children.



Published by Holy Heroes, LLC. All rights reserved. No part of this publication may be reproduced or used in any form or by any means—graphic, electronic, or mechanical, including photocopying, recording, or information storage-and-retrieval systems—without permission of the publisher.

Special thanks to Lauren Rupar for photo research and book design.

ISBN 978-1-936330-13-3   Printed in the U.S.A.

**HolyHeroes.com**

# A Note to Readers

The *Catechism of the Catholic Church* calls parents to be the "first heralds" to their children of the mysteries of the Faith, of all that is true and beautiful and good (CCC 2225).

We hope through these beautiful pictures created by some of the greatest artists of all time you can ignite the imaginations of your children to the truth and goodness of God and His Church.

Enjoy slowly, savoring phrase-by-phrase the Creed which has been handed down to us from God through His Apostles, introducing your future generations to the greatest mysteries they will ponder for the rest of their lives.

Gaze upon each image together and share the details you discover, contemplating the thoughts inspired by the words and the paintings. Like us, you'll often be surprised by the insights that flow from the hearts of little children.

May God bless you and yours!

Glory be to the Father, and to the Son, and to the Holy Spirit.
As it was in the beginning, is now, and ever shall be,
world without end. Amen.

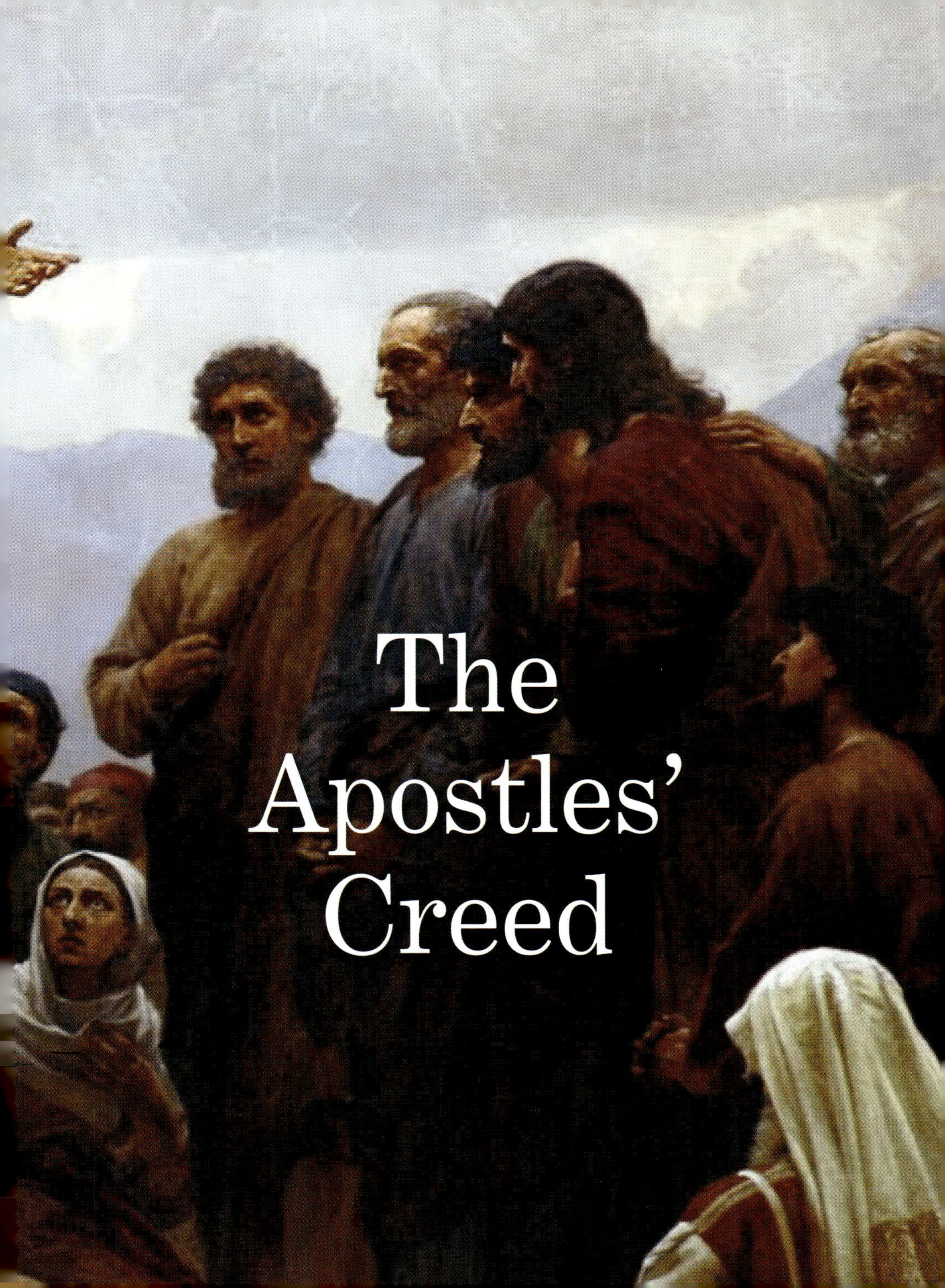
The
Apostles'
Creed

# I believe in God, the Father Almighty,

The Holy Trinity is three Divine Persons in one God.
God the Father is the First Person of the Holy Trinity.

# and earth,

God created all things—visible and invisible. The most important creatures God made are human beings and angels.

# and in Jesus Christ, His only Son, our Lord,

Jesus Christ is God. He is the Second Person of the Holy Trinity. Jesus also became a man and lived on Earth.

AVE MARIA GRACIA PLE
TECVM BENEDI
IN M
RIBVS E

# Who was conceived by the Holy Spirit,

Jesus Christ was made man by the power of the Holy Spirit
in the womb of the Blessed Virgin Mary.

# born of the Virgin Mary,

Jesus Christ was born on Christmas Day in Bethlehem. All three Divine Persons of the Holy Trinity chose the Blessed Virgin Mary to be the Mother of God.

# suffered under Pontius Pilate,

Pontius Pilate ordered the Roman soldiers to torture Jesus, but Jesus had done nothing wrong.

ישוע הנצרי מלך היהודים
ΙΗΣΟΥΣ ΝΑΖΟΡΑΙΟΣ ΒΑΣΙΛΕΥΣ ΙΟΥΔΑΙΩΝ
IESVS NAZARÆNVS REX IVDÆORVM

# was crucified,

Jesus loves you and me so much that He
allowed Himself to be nailed to the Cross for our sins.

# died

Jesus Christ died for our sins on Good Friday. He willingly offered up His life in order to open Heaven for us.

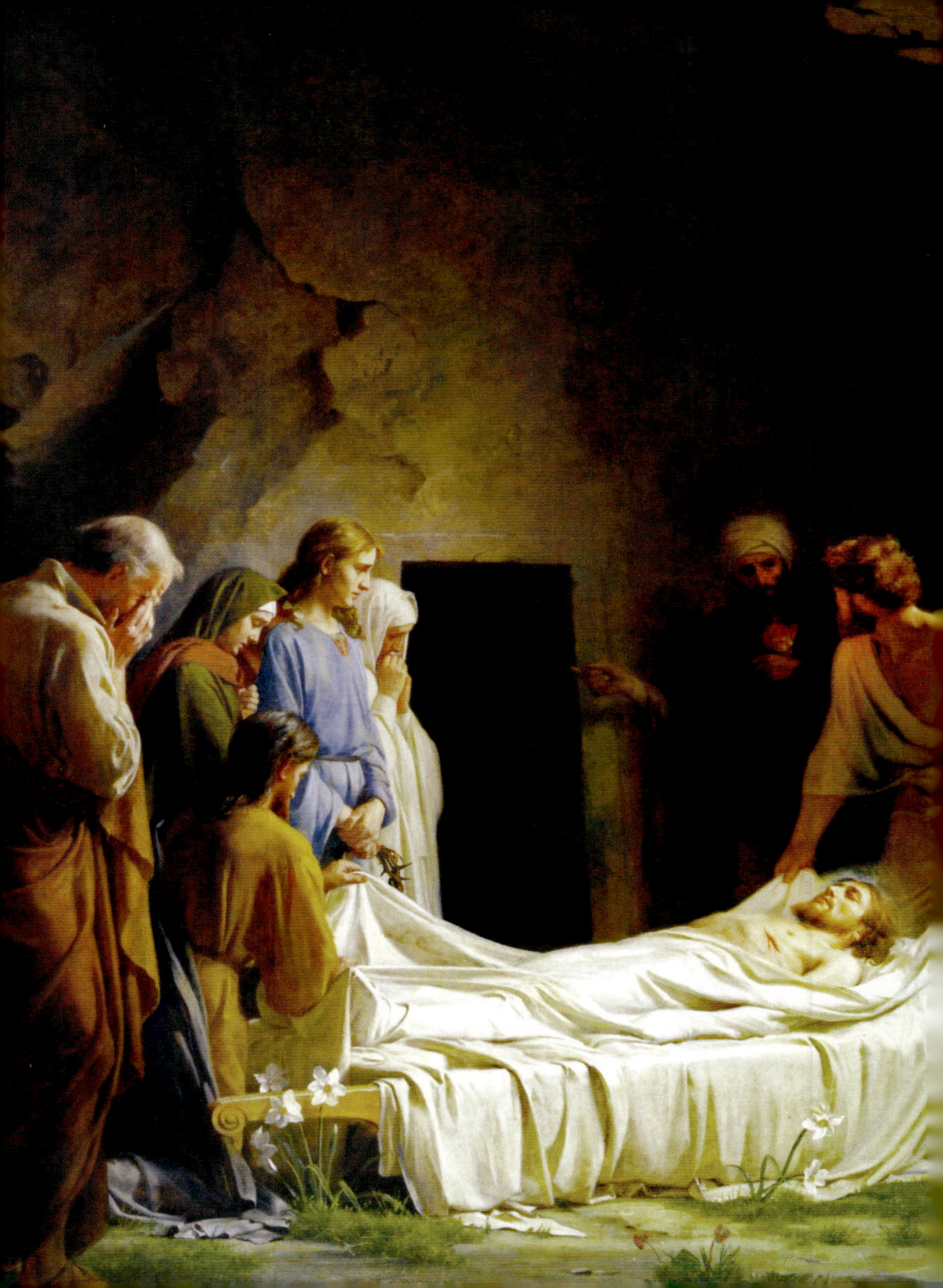

# and was buried;

Some of Jesus' friends took Him down from the Cross
and tenderly buried Him in a tomb.

# He descended into hell;

After Jesus died, He went to the place where the souls
of good people were waiting until He would
open Heaven for them.

# on the third day He rose again from the dead;

Jesus Christ rose from the tomb on Easter Sunday, the third day after His death on Good Friday.

# He ascended into Heaven,

Forty days after He rose from the dead, Jesus Christ ascended into Heaven. His disciples watched Him as He went up into a cloud.

# and is seated at the right hand of God the Father almighty;

As God, Jesus Christ is equal to God the Father, and as man,
He sits next to Him, in the highest place in Heaven.

# from thence
# He shall come
# to judge the living
# and the dead.

Jesus Christ will return on the last day of this world
to judge everyone who has ever lived.

# I believe in the Holy Spirit,

The Holy Spirit is God, the Third Person of the Holy Trinity.

# the holy catholic Church,

Jesus founded the Catholic Church to teach us and give us everything we need to have eternal life with Him in Heaven. The bishops are the successors of the Apostles.

# the communion of saints,

The communion of saints is the union of the faithful people here on Earth with the souls of those already in Heaven and the poor souls in Purgatory.

# the forgiveness of sins,

Before Jesus ascended into Heaven, He gave His Apostles the power to forgive sins. That power is handed down to our bishops and priests.

SECVND
VM·MAT
LIBER
GENERA
TIONIS
IESV
CHR
ISTI·F
FILII
DAVID
INITIV
EVANGE
LII IESV
CHRIST
NDV
MMAR
CVM·
SECVN
DVM
LVCAM
FVIT
IN·DIE
BY
HERO
DIS·RE
GIS·
SEC
VN
DVM·MAT·V
IOA
NMERB
IN·P
RINCIPI
AT·V

# the resurrection of the body,

At the end of this world, our bodies will be raised
and reunited with our souls, never again to be separated.

# and life everlasting.

All people will live either forever with God in Heaven
or forever separated from God in Hell.

# Amen.

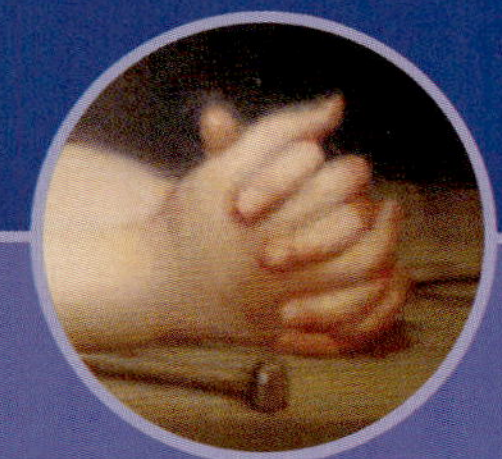

We say "Amen" to proclaim that we firmly believe
all that is contained in the Apostles' Creed.

# Picture Credits